SOME MAJOR EVENTS IN WORLD WAR II

THE EUROPEAN THEATER

1939 SEPTEMBER—Germany invades Poland Great Britain, France, Australia, & New Zealand declare war on Germany; Battle of the Atlantic begins. NOVEMBER—Russia invades Finland.

1940 APRIL—Germany invades Denmark & Norway. MAY—Germany invades Belgium, Luxembourg, & The Netherlands; British forces retreat to Dunkirk and escape to England. JUNE—Italy declares war on Britain & France; France surrenders to Germany. JULY—Battle of Britain begins. SEPTEMBER—Italy invades Egypt; Germany, Italy, & Japan form the Axis countries. OCTOBER—Italy invades Greece. NOVEMBER—Battle of Britain over. DECEMBER—Britain attacks Italy in North Africa.

1941 JANUARY—Allies take Tobruk. FEBRUARY—Rommel arrives at Tripoli. APRIL—Germany invades Greece & Yugoslavia. JUNE—Allies are in Syria; Germany invades Russia. JULY—Russia joins Allies. AUGUST—Germans capture Kiev. OCTOBER—Germany reaches Moscow. DECEMBER—Germans retreat from Moscow; Japan attacks Pearl Harbor; United States enters war against Axis nations.

1942 MAY—first British bomber attack on Cologne. JUNE—Germans take Tobruk. SEPTEMBER—Battle of Stalingrad begins. OCTOBER—Battle of El Alamein begins. NOVEMBER—Allies recapture Tobruk; Russians counterattack at Stalingrad.

1943 JANUARY—Allies take Tripoli. FEBRUARY—German troops at Stalingrad surrender. APRIL—revolt of Warsaw Ghetto Jews begins. MAY—German and Italian resistance in North Africa is over; their troops surrender in Tunisia; Warsaw Ghetto revolt is put down by Germany. JULY—allies invade Sicily; Mussolini put in prison. SEPTEMBER—Allies land in Italy; Italians surrender; Germans occupy Rome; Mussolini rescued by Germany. OCTOBER—Allies capture Naples; Italy declares war on Germany. NOVEMBER—Russians recapture Kiev.

1944 JANUARY—Allies land at Anzio. JUNE—Rome falls to Allies; Allies land in Normandy (D-Day). JULY—assassination attempt on Hitler fails. AUGUST—Allies land in southern France. SEPTEMBER—Brussels freed. OCTOBER—Athens liberated. DECEMBER—Battle of the Bulge.

1945 JANUARY—Russians free Warsaw. FEBRUARY—Dresden bombed. APRIL—Americans take Belsen and Buchenwald concentration camps; Russians free Vienna; Russians take over Berlin; Mussolini killed; Hitler commits suicide. MAY—Germany surrenders; Goering captured.

THE PACIFIC THEATER

1940 SEPTEMBER—Japan joins Axis nations Germany & Italy.

1941 APRIL—Russia & Japan sign neutrality pact. DECEMBER—Japanese launch attacks against Pearl Harbor, Hong Kong, the Philippines, & Malaya; United States and Allied nations declare war on Japan; China declares war on Japan, Germany, & Italy; Japan takes over Guam, Wake Island, & Hong Kong; Japan attacks Burma.

1942 JANUARY—Japan takes over Manila; Japan invades Dutch East Indies. FEBRUARY—Japan takes over Singapore; Battle of the Java Sea. APRIL—Japanese overrun Bataan. MAY—Japan takes Mandalay; Allied forces in Philippines surrender to Japan; Japan takes Corregidor; Battle of the Coral Sea. JUNE—Battle of Midway; Japan occupies Aleutian Islands. AUGUST—United States invades Guadalcanal in the Solomon Islands.

1943 FEBRUARY—Guadalcanal taken by U.S. Marines. MARCH—Japanese begin to retreat in China. APRIL—Yamamoto shot down by U.S. Air Force. MAY—U.S. troops take Aleutian Islands back from Japan. JUNE—Allied troops land in New Guinea. NOVEMBER—U.S. Marines invade Bougainville & Tarawa.

1944 FEBRUARY—Truk liberated. JUNE—Saipan attacked by United States. JULY—battle for Guam begins. OCTOBER—U.S. troops invade Philippines; Battle of Leyte Gulf won by Allies.

1945 JANUARY—Luzon taken; Burma Road won back. MARCH—Iwo Jima freed. APRIL—Okinawa attacked by U.S. troops; President Franklin Roosevelt dies; Harry S. Truman becomes president. JUNE—United States takes Okinawa. AUGUST—atomic bomb dropped on Hiroshima; Russia declares war on Japan; atomic bomb dropped on Nagasaki. SEPTEMBER—Japan surrenders.

WORLD AT WAR

Hiroshima

WORLD AT WAR

Hiroshima

By R. Conrad Stein

Consultant:
Professor Robert L. Messer, Ph.D.
Department of History
University of Illinois at Chicago Circle

 CHILDRENS PRESS, CHICAGO

The B-29 bomber *Enola Gay* (above) carried the atomic bomb that was dropped on Hiroshima.

FRONTISPIECE:
The youngsters lining up for kindergarten in modern Hiroshima have no memories of the day the atomic bomb fell on their city.

Library of Congress Cataloging in Publication Data

Stein, R. Conrad.
  Hiroshima.

  (World at war)
  Includes index.
  Summary: Traces events leading up to the 1945 bombing of Hiroshima and describes the horrible effects produced by the atomic explosion.
  1. Hiroshima-shi (Japan)—Bombardment, 1945—Juvenile literature.   2. Atomic bomb—Juvenile literature.   [1. Hiroshima-shi (Japan)— Bombardment, 1945.   2. Atomic bomb.   3. World War, 1939–1945—Japan]   I. Title.   II. Series.
D767.25.H6S83   1982   940.54'26   82-4538
ISBN 0-516-04797-3.   AACR2

1 2 3 4 5 6 7 8 9 10 R 91 90 89 88 87 86 85 84 83 82

PICTURE CREDITS:
UPI: Cover, pages 4, 6, 9 (right), 10, 11, 17, 19 (bottom), 22, 25 (top), 26, 29, 31, 32, 38, 39, 40
WIDE WORLD PHOTOS: Pages 9 (left top and bottom), 13, 14, 15, 18, 19 (top), 20, 33, 34, 37, 41 (top and left), 43, 44, 46
U.S. AIR FORCE PHOTO VIA UPI: Page 25 (bottom)
COLOUR LIBRARY INTERNATIONAL: Page 41 (right)

COVER PHOTO: The atomic bomb exploding over Hiroshima, Japan on August 6, 1945

PROJECT EDITOR
Joan Downing

CREATIVE DIRECTOR
Margrit Fiddle

On the Pacific island of Tinian, a B-29 bomber called the *Enola Gay* rested on an airstrip. Unlike the other bombers on the crowded airstrip, the *Enola Gay* was surrounded by a barbed-wire fence. Soldiers carrying machine guns patrolled the fence. The date was August 5, 1945. The very next day, the *Enola Gay* would fly mankind into a frightening new age.

War is sometimes called "the mother of invention." During wartime, men stretch their brains and their resources to build powerful weapons. The *Enola Gay* carried an atomic bomb, or A-bomb. It was by far the most destructive weapon ever created. Serious efforts to build this bomb had begun six years earlier with a conversation between two scientists.

In the summer of 1939, a scientist named Leo Szilard met with Albert Einstein. Einstein was such a famous scientist that even the president of the United States listened to him. Szilard told Einstein that he suspected the Germans were building an enormously powerful bomb based on uranium.

Einstein was a gentle genius. He understood the potential of atomic energy. But he never had dreamed about atomic power being used as a weapon. He realized instantly, however, that such a bomb could be built. If used against cities, an atomic bomb could kill thousands of people. A madman with such a bomb could terrorize the world.

Einstein wrote a famous letter to President Roosevelt. In it, he said that "extremely powerful bombs of a new type may thus be constructed. A single bomb of this type, carried by a boat and exploded in a port, might very well destroy the whole port, together with some of the surrounding territory."

Roosevelt read the letter and put it in a file. He was more concerned about the war that

Scientist Leo Szilard (above left) met with scientist Albert Einstein (left) in the summer of 1939 and urged Einstein to warn President Roosevelt (above) that the Germans might be building an atomic bomb.

seemed about to break out in Europe than he was about a bomb that sounded almost like a science-fiction weapon. Still, Roosevelt wondered what could happen if Hitler and the Nazi government actually built the kind of bomb Einstein described. Before filing Einstein's letter, Roosevelt wrote a note saying, "We must do something about this."

Nazi troops in Berlin drill in solid formation just before the outbreak of World War II in 1939.

As Roosevelt had feared, Europe exploded into war in 1939. While the war raged, evidence mounted that Germany was working on an atomic bomb. The Germans had taken over a heavy-water facility in Norway. Heavy water is needed to make a nuclear bomb. And the Germans were mining uranium in Czechoslovakia. An atomic bomb is fueled by uranium.

British and American scientists working in a secret laboratory under the bleachers at the University of Chicago's Stagg Field (above) achieved the first man-made nuclear chain reaction on December 2, 1942.

Roosevelt authorized American and British scientists to make experiments to determine whether or not an atomic bomb could be built. The most important of those experiments took place in Chicago on December 2, 1942. The scientists were working in a secret laboratory underneath the bleachers of a football field. There, they achieved the first man-made nuclear chain reaction. This proved that an atomic bomb could be built.

Roosevelt was afraid that Germany would develop the bomb first. Therefore, he made the building of an atomic bomb his most important project. Building the bomb would take money, scientists, and skilled workers. All these were in short supply. But the Americans would have the help of European scientists. Many of those scientists had fled Europe to escape Nazism.

To build the atomic bomb, scientists launched a super-secret program called the Manhattan Project. The Manhattan Project was so secret that not even the vice president knew it existed. The project cost more than two billion dollars, but no member of Congress ever voted to fund it. Thousands of people worked on the Manhattan Project. But only a handful knew what they were building.

While Manhattan Project scientists hurried into the atomic age, the war overseas took an ugly new direction. An all-out air war began that resulted in the killing of hundreds of thousands of civilians. Flights of bombers,

During the last few months of World War II, Allied fire bombs destroyed much of Hamburg, Germany (left) and Tokyo, Japan (right) and killed thousands of people.

sometimes a thousand strong, roared over Germany and Japan. Often they bombed military targets. Just as often, the mission of the bombers was to drop fire bombs on cities. Dresden, Germany was bombed, even though the city had little military value. Hamburg, Germany was destroyed by fire bombs, and thousands of people died. In one fire-bomb raid over Tokyo, 100,000 civilians lost their lives.

Above: A German buzz bomb plummets toward central London.
Below: German V-2 rocket damage south of London

The Axis countries used terror tactics, too. Germany launched V-1 buzz bombs and V-2 rockets against British cities. In the Pacific, Japanese suicide pilots crashed their planes into American ships. Both the Axis and the Allies waged total war.

On D-Day—June 6, 1944—the Allies invaded France. With the invasion forces was a small, highly secret unit called Alsos. Men of that unit traveled with the Allied army trying to determine just how far the Germans had progressed in building their atomic bomb. The

The secret Alsos unit went ashore with the invasion troops on D-Day (below).

Alsos unit radioed back some startling information. The Germans were not building an atomic bomb. They had been working on such a bomb early in the war, but had lost interest in the project.

In the United States, many Manhattan Project scientists sighed with relief. They thought the bomb was too horrible a weapon to be dropped on people. Now that they knew the Germans did not have an atomic bomb, they felt there was no reason to use those that were being built. Albert Einstein wrote President Roosevelt urging him to discontinue the American effort to build atomic bombs. But work on the atomic bomb continued.

In a lonely area of the New Mexican desert, the first atomic bomb was tested on July 16, 1945. Most scientists believed the bomb would have an explosive force of between five hundred and one thousand tons of TNT. But they were wrong. That first atomic bomb blew up with a force of twenty thousand tons of TNT. The

The first atomic bomb was tested in New Mexico on July 16, 1945 (above).

bomb exploded into a dazzling ball of orange light. Temperatures inside the ball were three times that of the sun. Desert sand beneath the blast melted and fused into glass. The hundred-foot-tall steel tower that had held the test bomb vanished without a trace.

17

One observer watching the explosion from a thick concrete bunker later wrote, "It was as though the earth had opened and the skies had split." Perhaps the most chilling comment came from Robert Oppenheimer, one of the inventors of the bomb. Oppenheimer quoted a line from an ancient book of Indian religion called the *Bhagavad-Gita*: "Behold. I have become death, destroyer of worlds."

On the island of Tinian, the B-29 called the *Enola Gay* raced its engines. It carried a single atomic bomb that was ten feet long, a little more than two feet wide, and weighed nine thousand pounds. Aside from its great size, it looked like an ordinary bomb.

This bomb is the same kind of weapon that was detonated over Hiroshima in August, 1945.

Above: The crew of the *Enola Gay*. Below: The officers of the *Enola Gay:*
Major Thomas W. Ferebee, bombadier; Colonel Paul W. Tibbets, pilot;
Captain Theodore J. Van Kirk, navigator; and Captain Robert Lewis, co-pilot.

At 2:45 A.M., August 6, 1945, the *Enola Gay*
taxied into a take-off position. Along the sides of
the airstrip, soldiers watched and photographers'
flashbulbs popped in the night. The men
stationed on Tinian knew that something
important was about to happen. But no one
knew exactly what.

Piloted by Colonel Paul Tibbets, the *Enola Gay*
(named after Tibbets' mother) rumbled down

the airstrip, picking up speed. Everyone held his breath because just the day before, four overloaded B-29s had crashed while trying to take off. Tibbets raced his bomber up to the speed of 180 miles an hour. But the great weight of the atomic bomb still held it down. Finally, with just a few feet of runway left, the B-29 lifted off the airstrip and soared like a giant silver eagle into the early morning sky.

Ahead of the *Enola Gay*, weather planes scouted the skies over Japan. The atomic bomb would be dropped on either Hiroshima, Niigata, Kokura, or Nagasaki. Hiroshima was the primary target, but the *Enola Gay* would fly to wherever the weather was clearest. A scout plane discovered few clouds over Hiroshima and radioed back the words: ADVICE: BOMB PRIMARY.

History's most awful weapon would strike first at Hiroshima.

Twenty years after the bomb, residents of a rebuilt Hiroshima were going about their business just as the people of this crowded city were doing on August 6, 1945.

In Hiroshima the people were just beginning a new day. Giggling children were scampering to school. Crowded streetcars were carrying workers to their jobs. The workers checked their watches, hoping they were not late. A few stretched their necks to see a large clock on a domed building downtown. But most of them knew that the large clock had stopped three days before. Since then, its hands had pointed to 8:15. How strange that the huge clock should have stopped at that time. On August 6, 1945, the atomic bomb exploded over Hiroshima at exactly 8:15 A.M., stopping every clock in the city at the same time.

These two views of Hiroshima show the total destruction
that resulted from the detonation of the atomic bomb.

High above downtown Hiroshima, the *Enola Gay*'s bombardier took aim at a bridge. The B-29 dropped its single bomb. And the world has never been quite the same again.

Seven hundred yards above Hiroshima, the bomb exploded like a huge flashbulb. Those directly below the blast vanished in the time it takes to blink an eye. Many left nothing more than white shadows on blackened sidewalks. Those shadows remained for years, burned into the sidewalks like ghostly photographs. No one knows how many people were instantly incinerated by the atomic bomb. But for those who survived the initial blast, the nightmare of Hiroshima was just beginning.

The fireball was followed by a thunderous shock wave. Buildings were crushed as if they had been smashed by the fist of an angry giant. People at home, in school, and at work were suddenly buried under walls and roofs. Fires broke out. Those people pinned under tons of debris died horribly.

Outside the collapsed buildings, the air was thick with a strange gray dust. It was hard to see more than a block in any direction. Twisted bodies, burned black, covered the ground. Shocked survivors seemed to be sleepwalking through the wreckage. Many were nearly naked. Scorched skin hung from their arms and legs.

One survivor, Mrs. Yasuko Nukushina, held her four-year-old daughter's hand. The girl kept saying, "Mama, I'm afraid." Mrs. Nukushina, in a daze, saw destroyed buildings and wounded people who looked like walking corpses. Her daughter's voice was strangely penetrating as she repeated, "Mama, I'm afraid. I'm afraid."

In the air, the *Enola Gay* sped toward home. Below, a city once had stood. Now it was gone. Paul Tibbets looked out the plane's window. He later claimed that "the surface [of Hiroshima] was nothing but a black, boiling barrel of tar." Co-pilot Captain Robert Lewis said, "My God, what have we done?"

The atomic bomb
left billows
of a newly
formed mushroom
cloud (left)
and a leveled
city (above).

25

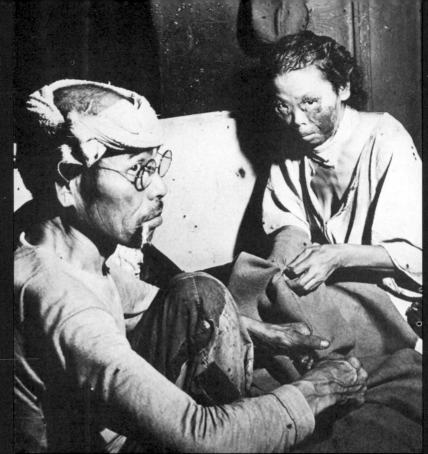

Survivors of the
Hiroshima blast,
covered with
ugly burns, were
cared for in a
damaged bank
building near the
center of town.

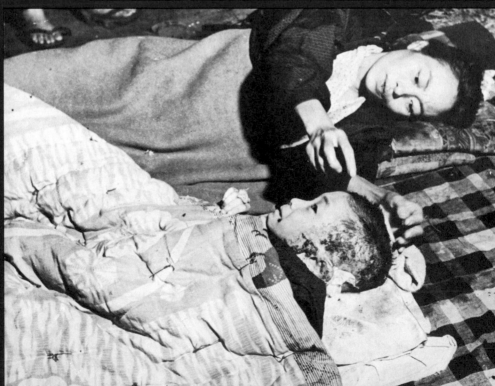

Many survivors have described the horror of Hiroshima. Perhaps the most chilling descriptions have come from the children of the city. They had nothing to do with the war. They suffered because the weapons of total war cannot tell the difference between a soldier and a frightened child.

Yoshihiro Kimura was in the third grade when the atomic bomb struck his city. Six years later he wrote a report about that day. In it he said, "Everything turned yellow in one instant. It felt the way it does when you get sunlight in your eye." Yoshihiro was knocked unconscious by the shock wave. He awoke to find his little sister standing above him. Ugly burns covered her body. Yoshihiro took his sister home to discover that his house had collapsed and his mother had been killed. Shocked, he went to the river for a drink. He wrote, "From upstream, a great many black and burned corpses came floating down the river. I pushed them away and drank the water." Later that night, the realization of his mother's death struck Yoshihiro. "I cried with all my soul. But no matter how hard I cry, my mother won't come back." And his sorrows were not over. "On the fifteenth of August, at about three o'clock, my sister finally died. . . . Apparently she was in agony, because she died with her eyes wide open." Even though his world had been shattered, Yoshihiro ended his report with these words: "I wouldn't hate any special person. . . . War is the enemy of everyone. If we can do away with war and if peace comes, I am certain that my mother in heaven will be happy."

Takako Okimoto was in the second grade when the bomb struck. She lost her entire family. In a letter, she wrote that "all of them, as a result of that atomic bomb, were struck down one after another. My oldest brother was never found after he left to work with the Labor

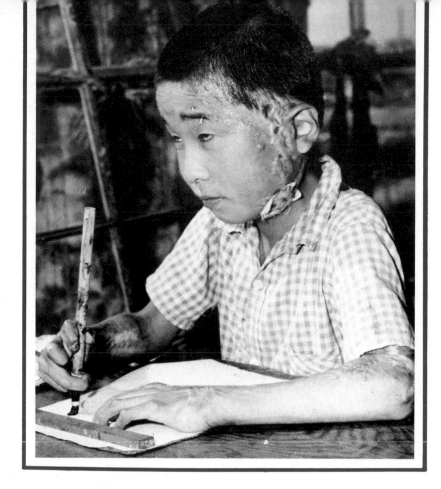

This child was about the same age as Takako Okimoto when the bomb fell. The awful memories, and the scars, will remain with both children all their lives.

Service group. My second brother's whole body was covered with burns and he died the next day. . . ." Two days later her mother died. "We cremated mother's corpse on the stony river bed. Here and there along the shore people were cremating corpses. And that evening, just after we arrived back at my uncle's house in the country with my mother's ashes, my big sister died." Takako's father died soon afterward, leaving her an orphan of the atomic bomb.

Hours after the atomic-bomb blast, Hiroshima was a city of dead and dying people. Many hospitals had been destroyed. The doctors and nurses who had survived set up aid stations on the outskirts of the city. From the center of the city, the victims of the bomb streamed to the aid stations. The lines of wounded people were unending. Doctors and nurses dressed wounds as well as they could.

Toward evening, doctors noticed that puzzling things were happening to the wounded. They began vomiting and having diarrhea. Many coughed up blood. Others were struck by a high fever. Their hair fell out in clumps. Red, green, and purple spots broke out on their skin. And they died. Many whose wounds did not seem severe died for unexplained reasons.

Scientists would later discover that radiation sickness was a deadly side effect of the atomic bomb. Inventors of the bomb had not guessed that their weapon would cause such awful sickness. But along with the fireball and the shock wave, the atomic bomb had released undreamed-of poisons that produced illnesses no doctor knew how to treat. Days, weeks, and years after the bomb exploded, its victims died from radiation sickness. Even today, Japanese people are dying from sicknesses caused by radiation from the atomic bomb.

Years after the atomic bomb was dropped on Hiroshima, studies were still being made to determine the effects of radiation on the victims.

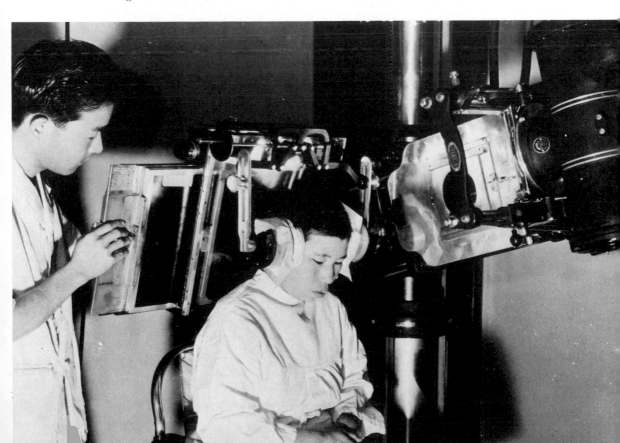

Tadashi Miki (above) lost his entire family, and his eyesight, on the day the atomic bomb was dropped on Hiroshima. Though he was no longer able to play his flute in an orchestra, he still found comfort in music.

No one knows the exact number of people the Hiroshima bomb killed. At least seventy thousand died on the first day. More than that number died later of wounds, burns, and radiation sickness. It is impossible to imagine the deaths of so many people. But it is possible to ask why the atomic bomb was dropped in the first place.

By the summer of 1945, Japan was already a defeated nation. Most of the ships of her once-powerful navy had been sunk. She had no way to defend herself against the swarms of American bombers that pounded her cities every day. Her few planes were being saved to send against the expected American invasion fleet. Her army had almost no gasoline for its tanks and trucks. The Americans occupied Okinawa, only ninety miles from the shores of Japan. And it seemed that the Russians would soon join the war against Japan and attack the Japanese army stationed in Manchuria.

By the summer of 1945, the Americans occupied Okinawa (shown below during a raid in October, 1944), only ninety miles from Japan.

President Truman (left) and Secretary of War Henry Stimson discuss the atomic bomb, which two days before had been dropped on Hiroshima.

So why use a weapon as terrible as the atomic bomb on an already defeated people? That question will be argued forever.

The order to drop the bomb came from President Harry Truman. He had become president after Roosevelt's death in April, 1945. Only after he became president did Truman learn that the United States was developing an atomic bomb. Truman appointed a special committee to advise him on how to use this new weapon. The committee was headed by Secretary of War Henry Stimson.

Stimson's committee argued about whether the atomic bomb should be dropped on a Japanese city. Several scientists wanted to demonstrate the power of the bomb by announcing that it would be dropped on an isolated part of Japan on a certain date. Such a demonstration explosion might scare the Japanese leaders into surrendering, and spare thousands of innocent lives. But other members of the committee were afraid the new bomb would fail to blow up. And perhaps the Japanese would shoot down the airplane carrying the demonstration bomb. Any number of things could go wrong with such a demonstration. So Stimson wrote the president, "We can propose no technical demonstration likely to bring an end to the war; we see no acceptable alternative to direct military use."

Certainly not everyone agreed with Stimson's committee. Leo Szilard, the scientist who had urged Einstein to write to Roosevelt in 1939, strongly disagreed. He headed a group of scientists who wrote Truman that any nation that uses an atomic bomb "may have to bear the responsibility of opening the door to an era of devastation on an unimaginable scale."

President Truman had been an artillery officer in World War I. In 1959 he told a student at Columbia University, "It [the atomic bomb] was just the same as getting a bigger gun than the other fellow had to win the war and that's what it was used for. Nothing else but an artillery weapon."

An artillery weapon that killed perhaps 200,000 people.

In 1945, most Americans supported their president's decision to drop the atomic bomb on Japan. Harsh war years harden people's feelings toward the death and suffering of others. In movie theaters, Americans cheered when they saw newsreels of Japanese cities turned into infernos by fire bombs. Inhumanity is the price all mankind pays for total war.

On August 9, 1945, President Truman gave a radio report to the nation on the war in the Pacific. That same day, another atomic bomb was dropped on Japan. The target of that bomb was the city of Nagasaki.

On August 6, 1945, President Truman made a radio speech announcing that a new and powerful bomb had obliterated Hiroshima. He demanded a Japanese surrender. If they did not surrender, he said, "they may expect a rain of death from the air, the like of which has never been seen on earth."

This mushroom cloud appeared over Nagasaki just after the atomic bomb was dropped on August 9, 1945.

After Hiroshima, events in the Pacific moved quickly. On August 8, Russia declared war on Japan. On August 9, another B-29 dropped an atomic bomb on the Japanese city of Nagasaki. That bomb killed at least forty thousand people on the first day.

Smoke still billowed over Nagasaki twenty minutes after the blast (middle picture). The resulting devastation (top picture) left thousands dead and injured, including this woman and child (above), and thousands more in need of temporary shelter in the ruins (left).

Huge crowds lined the streets as Emperor Hirohito (right) began his trip home after visiting the shrine of his ancestors to report the defeat of Japan by the Allies.

On August 14, the Japanese government accepted American terms for surrender.

In Tokyo, the Japanese people heard a radio address they never dreamed they would hear. Their emperor told them they must "bear the unbearable." The people of Japan worshipped their emperor like a god. No Japanese had ever heard his voice before, and only a few had ever seen his face. But now the emperor was on the radio telling the Japanese people that their war was over.

On September 2, 1945, about three weeks after newspaper headlines in the United States shouted the news of Japan's surrender, formal surrender ceremonies took place aboard the U.S.S. *Missouri* in Tokyo Bay.
Right: Lieutenant General Sir Arthur Percival (left) and Lieutenant General Jonathan Wainwright (second from left), both of whom had been prisoners of the Japanese, were on hand to witness the signing of the documents.
Left: Mamoru Shigemitsu (at desk) signed on behalf of the emperor of Japan and General Douglas MacArthur, Supreme Allied Commander, signed for the Allies.

Perhaps the atomic bomb helped bring an end to the war. But someday, perhaps, nuclear bombs will be used in a war that will bring an end to life on the earth. Today hydrogen bombs exist that are thousands of times more powerful than the bomb that fell on Hiroshima. Using such weapons in war would be insane. No one side could win a nuclear war. Yet the United States and Russia continue building bombs that are more and more powerful. The two countries now have the power of about one million Hiroshima bombs in their arsenals. And Britain, France, China, and India have nuclear bombs. Some experts believe that still other countries own nuclear bombs, but are keeping them a secret. By the end of the century, twenty countries could have nuclear weapons.

Hiroshima today is a busy, modern city. But reminders of that terrible day in 1945 still

Hiroshima today (above) is a prosperous, modern city.

remain. On the concrete steps of the Sumitomo
Bank, the shadow of a man incinerated by the
atomic bomb is still visible. Eerie shadows of
people who vanished into fire once were
imprinted on many downtown streets and
walkways. Now only the one on the bank steps
remains as a reminder of the awesome power of

Thousands packed Hiroshima's Peace Memorial Park (right) during a ceremony that marked the twentieth anniversary of the first atomic bomb to be dropped on human beings.

the atomic bomb. The skeleton of a domed building still stands near the river. It is the only remaining example of a building damaged by the bomb. In Peace Park, a graceful arch contains a list of the names of all those known to have died because of the bomb. Even today, new names are being added to that list.

Visitors often weep when they walk past one famous Hiroshima monument. It is called the Children's Monument. Put up in 1958, it was dedicated to the children of Hiroshima who died because of the bomb. It was inspired by the death of a girl named Sadako Sasaki.

Sadako was two years old when the bomb exploded about a mile from her home. She seemed unhurt, but when she was in the sixth grade, Sadako became sick with leukemia. Leukemia is a cancer of the blood. It was one of the many diseases spread by radiation from the atomic bomb. In the hospital, Sadako wrote in her diary, "I don't want to die." She was very sick, but she amazed doctors and nurses because she always laughed and sang when her classmates visited her. She started to make little paper figures of cranes. An old saying in Japan holds that if a sick person makes 1,000 paper cranes he will become well. But Sadako did not live long enough to make 1,000 paper cranes. She had finished 964 when she died. Her classmates completed the remaining cranes and they were placed with Sadako in her coffin.

Today, on top of the Children's Monument, a statue of Sadako Sasaki stands tall. She is holding a crane in her outstretched arms. At the base of the statue are carved the words: "This is our cry, this is our prayer: peace in the world."

A statue of
Sadako Sasaki,
holding a crane
in her
outstretched
arms, stands
on top of the
Children's
Monument in
Hiroshima.

Index

Page numbers in boldface type indicate illustrations.

About the Author

Mr. Stein was born and grew up in Chicago. At eighteen he enlisted in the Marine Corps where he served three years. He was a sergeant at discharge. He later received a B.A. in history from the University of Illinois and an M.F.A. from the University of Guanajuato in Mexico.

Although he served in the Marines, Mr. Stein believes that wars are a dreadful waste of human life. He agrees with a statement once uttered by Benjamin Franklin: "There never was a good war or a bad peace." But wars are all too much a part of human history. Mr. Stein hopes that some day there will be no more wars to write about.